Bright Soil, Dark Sun

poems by

Samuel T. Franklin

Finishing Line Press
Georgetown, Kentucky

Bright Soil, Dark Sun

ACKNOWLEDGMENTS

Versions of some poems in this collection first appeared in the following publications:

Branches: "Greening"
Down in the Dirt Magazine: "Old Railtrack"
Eunoia Review: "Watermelon Surplus" and "Tree Bones"
Fickle Muses: "Divinity"
Flying Island: "Winter Mornings on 17th Street"
HoosierLit: "The House on Iowa Street"
Indiana Voice Journal: "Spring Break 2010," "Coffee Nights," and "Some Summer Work"
Indianapolis Review: "When the Storm Moves On"
M Review: "The Light at the End of the Universe"
Mobius: "After Mythology"
Rabid Oak: "Alan Kurdi" and "Basement Apartment"
Riggwelter: "In a Previous Life" and "Sisyphus at the Summit"
Scarlet Leaf Review: "At the Site of Fort Sackville," "I Have Seen the Dead," "The House on Clark Street," and "Killing the Ants"
Third Wednesday: "Driving on an August Evening," "On a Ferry for Beaver Island, MI," and "As Things Are"

I'd also like to thank Kaylin Brian and Courtney Diles for their keen eyes and excellent suggestions. Thank you.

Publisher: Leah Maines
Editor: Christen Kincaid
Cover Art: Samuel T. Franklin
Author Photo: Samuel T. Franklin
Cover Design: Elizabeth Maines McCleavy

Printed in the USA on acid-free paper.
Order online: www.finishinglinepress.com
          also available on amazon.com

Author inquiries and mail orders:
Finishing Line Press
P. O. Box 1626
Georgetown, Kentucky 40324
U. S. A.

Table of Contents

I. Radiance and Shadows

II. The Language of Discord

III. Politics, Gods, and Other Nightmares

IV. Rejoining the Spiral

For Jenna

I.

Radiance and Shadows

City Aspect

There's a cyclist who comes zipping
            around the corner as I'm driving west
on 3rd Street his dreadlocks like
            puddled gold like a fireball like
a heart attack as he speeds through
            the intersection and car horns
float like a symphony and his
            palms are like white doves
floating open beside him empty

            as the concrete shadows
where morning makes a wide
            left turn and its tires squeal
in the parking garage around
            orange construction cones and
the sun is still a dream and
            the dream is still awake and
work is calling and morning's
            breath is snow-cold and
in the steel girder skeleton-cage
            a universe explodes
from the welder's work
            flash-white blue
and sparking freshet and how
            it burns and flares and
arcs down to the sidewalk
            by his brown and frosty boot

that shuffles beneath a booth
            with a blues guitar slicing
radio speakers and trays
            and clay cups and frycooks
and cutlery clatter and rattle
            and outside the bars are
closing the moon is spent and
            no one's on the roads now
and the waitress is pouring

three in the morning her arm
strong and poised and caffeine
        streams down and steams up
a statue for a perfect moment.

Some Summer Work

Storefront attic I'd ladder up into,
        breathing straw-rot air though
wet bandanas and crunching bird

        bones beneath my boots. Sunless,
shapeless, dark as the mice turds
        or my snot at the end of the day,

dirt-clogged, thick as a slug.
        I'd knife moldering cardboard
until the metal siding sang

        with heat and they'd call up
for me to come down, back
        and forth like the load and unload

of some gasoline summers later,
        trash-pick and grass-cut and dawn
already a mist of heat reflecting

        off my bike spokes. And now
the shimmer-heat afternoons
        off work, unpaid and pulling

for pleasure tangled vines from warped
        wood, splitting stumps
and goading the yuccas to grow and glint

        in wet sun like the rainy stones
I've set out to dry, memories
        unearthed and warming in sunset.

Coffee Nights

The Coffee Grounds—Terre Haute, Indiana

They'd pin me in line
    and have a Hammerhead register-ready—

espresso sunk in a mug of black tar
    that caught the edge of sundown.

The bars would light up down the street,
    and I'd be a shadow at the corner table,

taming grad school with caffeine and bagels.
    Mortared, makeshift, a snug castle

for writing midnight away,
    the barista lost in *Moby Dick*,

headshop kids tapping packs of cigs,
    a student sharing hot tea with her term paper.

Other nights I'd be there
    with Heaney and Sandburg in my pocket,

reading pen-and-pencil lines into a microphone,
    my voice an uneven murmur,

a shaky beat gone out to shuffle
    with the townpoets and the rhyme-folk,

their own chant-and-cadence mystic
    in the coffesteam room, the aroma

char-dark and bitter, and low light shadowing
    crumble-brick walls written over

with poems and names and love-notes left
    on Terre Haute's runic skin.

River: Wabash

Mud-lovely, brown as supple leather,
        smooth as a bluegill's sleek belly,
rabbit-twist of choppy froth kicking
        banks thick with stone and roots.
I never dove in or drank of it, cupped
        it in my palms and lifted it to catch
the sun there and turn the well
        of my hands orange as water you could
find seeping from swales or in roadside
        ditches. No branching tributaries sliced
a path down my throat, silted my innards
        with nitrogen or bug-killer, that swift
and ink-thick water, death-heavy
        for Gulf fish who drown in its lifeless
surge. And its kin-flow from our tap
        in a little shotgun apartment on
Walnut Street, the rush of city-gush
        through rusty and leaden pipes,
the peaceful leak-drip near the faucet
        neck, the little necklace of
white crust that collected there. I let
        it settle when we first moved in,
poured a clear glass straight from
        the city, saw the sediment swirl
in the bottom after some minutes,
        a black little tornado, playful
debris, like the battered remains
        of sunken barges and paddleboats
dancing in the river's unseen depths.

River: Beneath

There were dark currents
　　　　roaming like blind horses

through glistening
　　　　chutes beneath our Clayton house, and

when it rolled
　　　　like a cascade from the tap

and into kitchen cups
　　　　and then into our bellies

and blood—I didn't
　　　　know then how good it was,

clean-tasting and light
　　　　as a rainbow. When we all left

for good, we went with
　　　　canned jams and jellies, the fruit

grown in the backyard
　　　　and mother-made. That was the last

of childhood's harvest
　　　　I knew, and the last of the water

that cleaned me and
　　　　quenched thirsts and raised apple trees

and asparagus and corn
　　　　from the soil like the bony hands

of a green god
　　　　slowly resurrected from root and sod.

The House on Iowa Street

Limestone-boned, its land leveled
       with gas-lamps limning the night

and horse-hooves clopping
       the thoroughfare. Stone

pillars guarding entry up the long,
       curling cat-tail driveway, ceaseless

shade-green acre that went back
       and back and back. Tiger-orange

persimmons, peonies pink and white
       near the woodfort our father built,

garden all corn-gold
       and strawberry-plump. And in

the apple grove, Japanese beetles
       summer-clustered, the coppery-green

feasters brighter
       than the basement sprickets

skittering in the cellar. I avoided
       those sunless rooms for years,

convinced ghosts swam
       in the lower pipes, funeral home

spirits who paced at night
       up all the creaking steps

of childhood's light-filled gauze—
       where a piano radiates evening music

like a furnace throwing heat,
       our mother's notes in wood-walled rooms

where I sometimes still dwell
       just before waking, sleeping

in past patterns, the music echoing
       from emptiness like half-heard

calls to come home, child,
       come home,

the sun
       is bedding down.

Thrombosis

Pollen-fire smokes
        me guts-first,

skin kettle-hot while
        little bombs roll

along my lungs' curvatures,
        and autumn reshapes

my heart around
        a knife blade.

A name that isn't
        mine sweats out

from behind folders
        and insurance forms.

Double-shift nurse rattles
        close, her hair black

as molasses, syrup-thick,
        stack of clipboard papers

in hand. A foot in a chair
        has a bent blue toe, a woman

stares with red
        mineshaft eyes

and does not move.
        A name that still

isn't mine clogs
        time and space.

Coughs, cries. I am fire
        in a room of broken

things and stagnant
        light, but a fire

is whole. My knife twists.
        I settle around it

like teeth
        around a bite.

Winter Mornings on 17th Street

The sky tumbles to Earth and shatters
to ice. Snow folds like colorless oceans
and shifts, greedy, across naked trees.

The creek shines clear and clean
as wiped porcelain. A man in dark wool
studies the frozen currents,

drops twigs and pine needles on the ice
and tries to conjure some prophecy of spring.
Wind slips subtle as a thorn

through jackets and gloves.
I do not know this city,
and the ravens are quiet.

The man in dark wool stands,
hopeless, the twigs piled at his feet,
burned by invisible fire.

What a Poet Cannot Understand

Cool tile
under toe,
and silk
slips down

like epiphany.
Fat spider
dangles, struck
matchhead,

burnt-looking
weaver eye-level
and twitching
nose-length

from nostrils.
It rides
my breath-waves,
drawn in

toward teeth's
dark cave
like truth
infecting lies.

Eight against
two—we
watch us
watching us.

My inner
poet tries
for meaning.
My inner

spider knows
none exists.
It slips
down dark

pipes and
spins a net
before
it drowns.

Basement Apartment

Boiler is hissing in the corner
       like a time-bomb ready to blow,

and the dishes are black crusts
       in a sink full of spiderwebs

and a dirty line of soap scum. It's evening,
       and red sunlight cuts

through the slit windows
       and drips over everything. Bill

nods to the back room and tells me
       that's where they found the boy, his brains

all over the walls like someone
       had thrown a bowl of oatmeal, cold gun

on the floor. Been there for weeks.
       Neighbors thought rats had died

in the walls, the smell was so bad
       when it finally slipped up the winter pipes

and nestled into the furniture.
       Bill tells me I won't hear about it

from the neighbors, at least the ones
       who might have heard the muffled shot

if they knew what to listen for. Doesn't mean
       it didn't happen. I ask him

for the boy's name, but he can't remember.
       Doesn't mean he didn't die. There's

a guitar in a corner chair, neck as broken
        as a wrung chicken. I won't let

these things slip. Even if I ever forget,
        doesn't mean they didn't happen.

Evening in April

A backyard is blue with rain.
Clouds press their steely lips against

shingles and leaves, the trickling
of the world steady as a faucet drip. Glum

puddles grow into cancers, slip back
through time and devour my grandparents

from the insides. I envision age seventy:
skin spalted with carcinomas. Prostate purpling

slowly into an eggplant. A clarinet mourns
nearby, weaves dark silk between

shagbark branches and boxelder fingers. Faces
peer from every spreading wildflower,

dusky spring-glow recasts each grass-thatch
into newness and never-knowns. Light

drops through the clouds like
a downed plane, sets every bulb of rain

on fire. I see my body in a year,
or five, or ten—a darkness in a pillar of flame,

a still safekeeping for bullets, or sidewalk-fallen
like a rot-hearted tree in a forest. Eyes

open, blue, and blessed to never
see another evening like this.

The Light at the End of the Universe

Not the bioluminescence
        of fireflies pulsing around the maple

out back, nor evening sunfire
        flying through purple dusk, but

the weak electric glow
        on unmoving brown fur.

A young rabbit. Huddled
        in the paintbrush shadows

beneath my workbench.
        Dead. Stretched on its side,

unbloodied, unbroken, perfect
        save for its stillness. Trapped

overnight, unseen in darkness
        when I pulled the door down

and killed whatever light
        had lit its small eyes. I try

to taste its terror, panting
        in hot blindness until its heart

seized. Or maybe choosing
        to dive into the lightlessness

that lingers in all living
        things, embracing its own unknown

instead of squealing
        and screaming with only spiders

and dust to hear it. I lifted
        its thinness and touched the cold

fur and carried it outside
        to birdsong and humming wind,

the thick knot of vines
        climbing the fence. I nestled

it into the green, and in
        its eye was a pale and dim cloud

like the light of stars
        long dead softly fading through space.

II.

The Language of Discord

I Have Seen the Dead

They hold blue fire in boxes
   they speak with their fingers

they hunker around their bonfires
   flames fork the wings of their shadows

they dream of ascending
   into marbled skyscrapers

and signing their names over
   and over and over in gold

nesting in wide cool houses
   and sunset bricks and vast grasses

see their fingerbone wages
   see them drifting from windows

the rustle of stained aprons
   crumpled in corner chairs

the blood-tired sighs
   the loans of money promised

the promise of money loaned
   hear their footsteps hear them breathe

see the gravestones on their backs
   see the shovels in their hands.

Spring Break 2010

Pine needles prick our lungs
and auger moons hunker skyward
these woodstove nights with frost licking

windows, bodies sleeping in church pews
and toolshed bunks and burrowed
in branches and dead leaves, cold mountain

wind breaking on black wool knit. We hack
trees free from their honeysuckle cages. My
boots are yellow in black mud, my skin

is milk in the forest's dark tea, and
the wind that haunts this stolen Cherokee
land binds me and whispers of hung chiefs

and shaved braids, of split tongues
and Sequoyah's syllabic light, one word
of which, *nunv,* potato, was written

on a clothespin and given
to me, the small spelling a reminder
of the cave-country dwellers rifled

from their homes and whose ghosts
still bone-march and death-stagger
down a long and bloodstained trail of tears.

       Once we were mighty,

the tribesman speaks,
face red against the bonfire
and the stars smoking above us,

       Once we were sun-blessed,
       and now we're homeless, jobless,
       swallowing poverty and McDonald's

and infomercials for hours
because we were conquered
and are being conquered,
but we nourish our ghosts
so they'll sing to us their stories,
and we will always, always remember.

A dusty jar of collected words,
a dying that will not end, a life
that refuses to die, a mountain

that will not weep,
a people like a shattered fist
that grips, still, and pulls.

The Beauty

The hands that dipped
  their tips into baptismal holiness
are the same that claimed Tecumseh
  in the red swamps after Moraviantown,
stripped the flesh from the body
  for razor strops. And the fists
that hoisted Washington's flag
  when Cornwallis capitulated America
tightened Nat Turner's noose
  and drove the nails for fiery crosses.

This moment
  beneath a cold American moon,
a child dreams of holy light
  illuminating shimmering black roses,
their petals glowing
  like polished marble. When
the thorns pierce flesh,
  the child cries and wakes, dream-pain
in them like a sharp tooth, but
  remembers only the beauty,
the beauty,
  the beauty.

Double Eagle in a Vigo County Pawnshop

Like a fire in the desert of my palm,
a cold comet lifted from the cage

of a Hoosier pawnshop's coin case—
double eagle, golden St. Gaudens. The shadows

of its glow black, I imagined, as
Mansa Musa's kingly brow, or

fur-lined broadcloth wrapped around
Jakob Fugger's shoulders. Millenia

ago, stars exploded and poured
their molten hearts into the red cradle

of the Sierra Nevadas, the American River,
where millions of cracked hands

would fight to pan sunlight from water,
soft yellow nuggets that gleamed like the teeth

of murdered Aztec gods. Endless toll-roads,
sunset mesas blasted apart for train routes,

nerve gas, burger joints, atomic bombs,
empty bank accounts—all caught and bought

by the little metal fortune in my palm,
the color of the limit of human love.

The shopkeeper eyed me until
I put it back, that chip of history, hint

of minted bullion men have killed
and died to own, to touch, to taste—

nothing but a lump of molded ore
from veins mined in dirty caves.

As Things Are

Pink and glistening umbilicus
writhes blindly among the peony roots.

Tiny, scarlet-feathered dinosaurs
pull it wriggling from the soil.

I grin and bare my pacu teeth
and watch with my chimpanzee eyes.

When the Storm Moves On

It doesn't die. It just slips
        into a different robe,

one cut from spring-blue skies,
        but lined with shattered houses.

It walks among the people,
        unseen, a cheerful gust twirling

its fingers through their hair,
        before stripping in the middle

of the street, stamping its feet,
        and shrieking that it's had enough

and that everyone, *everyone*
        is about to be broken.

Circling

Nights the road brings
     you fists of lightning
and something dark
     with rain-clatter windshield
and poncho ghosts
     by mile-marker graves
with cocked thumbs
     to tell you keep
going you're on
     the path you chose.

Nights you've lost
     you're lost in deep
rumbling thunders
     red as neon portents
the diesels circle
     like sharks around
Taco Bells like
     flabby tigers around
shithole bars like
     hurt and furious
ogres sucking
     dirt from scabs
all shouting
     death to pigs.

Nights moonscapes loom
     empty shopping malls
like fossil teeth
     still biting or
empty boots
     walking themselves
behind the dumpster
     and in passing
streetlamp fire
     you can see
someone sleeping

on a bench red
as a stovetop burning
in the careful shadows
of an abandoned house.

Old Railtrack

Old railtrack sweating
        forgotten rust at sunset—
so strange in this train-city,
        like ditch-roses.

Sunfried asphalt, broken
        windows, plywood patches
of foreclosed houses,
        the long ghostcalls

of distant trains through
        tree-claws and the running
tunnel piped beneath
        those junk-tracks, cold

buried chute where
        shadows choked sunlight, where
graffiti scrawlings crawled
        beneath my flashlight,

rhymed names and
        named crimes and jungle
drawings of the monsters
        that lurk on the edge of town

with syringes, with
        red eyes, with rotten dreams.
Quotes of dead
        poets, cannibal longings

and wish-prayers
        the lonely roamers all
offered to the void,
        drawn to gleaming

metal bones, weed-rust,
        the world and what haunts

beneath it blending in
      bitter harmony.

Night Snow

Cold-quiet
       blue frost smothering the night

summer's grief crystallized
       your lashes long and white

stillness
       of the ragged storefront blanket

thin huddle of boots
       skinny arms in a stained surplus jacket

and the only lights shake
       behind curtained windows

soft and liminal constellations
       by which nightbirds and ghosts

can find their way
       back home.

His Name's Mark, He's Got No Shirt, No Shoes, No Home, He's on the Corner of Seventh and College with a Cardboard Sign and Sweating in the Hot Noon for Pennies Thrown into a Battered Old Hat

But you're looking at white tree petals
dusting the sidewalk and filling
the cloudless spring
with their spore-sex and sweet
pollen and the sun
is a raging laughing child knowing
warmth for the first time and
shop windows and passing windshields throw
its fire back into the air
like sky lanterns loosed
upon thermal currents
and you're blind to everything
but the unfolding life-season
the scintillating mouth-watering smell
of grilled meat and baking bread and
the cool thought of beer in frosty glasses fills
your stomach and empties your wallet
because the very air is a rhyme
and spring wraps its legs around you and sings
and the meanness of the world
is in some other place
far, far away.

Alan Kurdi

Fishbone bed and a grave
of sand. A dead crab washes ashore,

a plastic bottle bobs in seafroth
and green weeds. This is no place

for a boy. Someone will come.
A gull inflates like a lung

and floats on salty air. This
is no place for a boy.

Watermelon Surplus

Dead of summer, I'm aproned
and sweating at my seasonal retail job,
stacking cucumbers, stocking salads,

slicing potato sacks—golden, red, russet.
We get a watermelon surplus—we truss it

all off the truck, extra pallets packed
with cardboard bins bursting with fruit.
We heave them through backrooms

to the selling floor, all those globes
of green goodness, round, ripe lobes.

Boss balks. Supplier oversight,
shipping more than specified,
but we can't send them back now.

Can't sell them either, he frowns.
They'll drive our price down,

we'll take a hit. No discounts, no donations.
Not my rule—I just enforce it.
You know what to do.

We jack the pallets and roll across the floor
through the stock rooms, to the compactor,

its cracked door a portal to the rancid reek
of curdled milk, blackened bananas and rotting meat.
We sling in the melons—

firm-fleshed, picnic-perfect. They smash
and burst, seeds and pink slush, food turned to trash,

and we contemplate the water now wasted growing them,
gas guzzled to drive them from Georgia,
the insane economics of a world

where food is better in the dumpster
than alleviating someone's hunger.

The Day

Another apron day. Pallet-runner stares at me
from backroom mirrors, reflective steel

of deep-chested sinks and pineapple corers.
Long of hair, short of wits,

exploding from boredom
and dick-brained scenarios

about the quick-fingered cashier
with ankles smooth as grapes.

On the floor, I cull the mold
from peaches and rotting bananas,

and a dead man steps beside me,
skin-on-bone man with cobweb hair

and paper skin and cancer
like a stone in the fruit of his eye,

and I can conjure still the sick-sweet smell
of death curling around him,

and he smiles beneath his white cowboy hat
and says to me

How old are you, banana boy?

I tell him

Eighteen

He coughs and says

Eighteen. Soon
a wife will find you,

a life will wind you
down its path. You
will be judged
by what woman you love,
what car you drive,
so don't mess up. Do it right.
Go to college, earn some money,
live strong, live proud. Live happy.
That's all you gotta do. Don't forget it.

And the dead man winks,
takes a banana, turns away.

I am haunted. His words, his eyes,
the smell. They follow me

to the stock cooler and potato bins
and the grapes that no longer

remind me of that cashier's ankles,
and I almost do not see

before I put my hand on it
the crouching black widow

splaying eight nightmare legs
atop the fruit box on my cart,

its red warning and its empty eyes
a soundless and piercing scream.

I drive home near midnight,
and the road is cool and empty,

and the moon is a scythe
above the corn flats,

and I'm thinking of my soft bed
and my cracked hands

and the dead man
and the spider hiding in the grapes,

and blue and red lights are tilting
in the dark of the world,

an ambulance, police cars,
the right lane coned off to traffic.

An empty and useless gurney. A busted
motorcycle, its parts all over tarmac.

A man hosing wet, red streaks
off the street, and someone shoveling

messy chunks of some unmoving thing
into thick, black bags. And

the night turns
sick-sweet, turns sour,

turns rotten
as bananas blackening on a shelf.

At the Site of Fort Sackville

We came howling down the highway,
brash war songs like honey on our lips.
Histories of genocide and tropical suns

scorching darker skin—the crowns
we were born into. In Indiana's southern hills,
we could imagine wind guttering

through dusky grasses, wild bison
and the skinners who scraped their pelts
and stole tongues red as the fire of Mars

come nightfall. In Vincennes, we paled
before George Rogers Clark's bronze eyes,
the Wabash-wader, hero of the frozen war

who claimed untamed prairies and rivers,
whose legacy shone brightest where meth now creeps
on shoeless feet down dark Hoosier alleys,

his name a ghost on cracked lips. Would
he have done it all again, traded blood
for a life's glory, if he could see today

what he helped shape? See all the sweat
and fighting and death in one dusty
paragraph in a bored student's book?

The sun mushroomed to the horizon
when we left, dipped us in gold
that dulled to dirty tin,

and twilight fell upon the Wabash
like the shattered walls of a captured fort
whose boundaries no one will ever remember.

After Mythology

You've found stones the shape of your fist
by grey lakewaters, quartz studs

like knuckles and curled thumbs
of bony granite. Fear burns cleanly

these days, bright as oxygen and
just as cheap. A buddy tells you he mistrusts

anyone who says to mistrust anyone
over thirty. You don't tell him

you mistrust all the lost beings
who dwell in high places—words fall

and scatter into unknowable flocks
from such heights, and just how

can a god or a guy with a bad combover
see what life's like in America's Midwest,

even if they're both in government jobs and
presumably know how to use Google?

Nevermind that you're almost
thirty yourself, been almost thirty

for years, ever since you could talk.
You know folks who rub ash

into their skin like it was soap,
who'd live their lives in a scullery hell

just so they could complain about
tending the coals. They trace footpaths

in the grime of their skin, list names
of people whose lives they'd like to possess,

and forget that we're all questing
to recover the same sacred objects:

broken housekeys, dishonored names,
hearts that stay true in windy darkness.

But none of us have maps or wings
or signposts—all the territory is new

in a world that refreshes every second,
and we'll only ever have the tools

given to any traveler wandering after dark:
our feet, a door, a thin and moonlit road.

The House on Clark Street

I.
There are deer who nibble the young hostas
unfurling in our front yard. They lope
on silent hooves before sunbreak
while mist breathes from cool earth.
They are shadows moving among shadows,
gone soon as they are seen.

II.
Coffee black as the dirt beneath my shovel.
We bury the last of the student loans
beneath yuccas and lilies, cover it up
with soil and brown roots and sing a blues song
over its grave. We bite into thick lamb steaks
like we've never used our teeth.

III.
Something stirs at night
in wind bending the treetops, in the gloom
beyond the gold sodium glare. It echoes
in the cough of rusty mufflers, mumbles dark lullabies
up the sidewalk just out of sight. A sound of feet,
shifting, dragging, drifting.

IV.
There is an afterlife in the long morning shadows
with indigo lupine by the front window and fat
honey-makers buzzing lazily. An idyll
we think we deserve. My lungs eat the air. I feel
the wind in my blood and know I am not dead
and have earned nothing.

     Fortune is luck,

I tell the grass. A cloud swallows the sun.

V.

The deer dodge trucks in early starlight.
Quiet hooves sink into mud dark as the hole
in the heart of a dream. From the shade
of the magnolia's pink blossoms, I see
a man with a ragged backpack moving down the road,
the ceaseless clap of feet
like someone knocking at the door.

III.

Politics, Gods, and Other Nightmares

Before Prometheus Gave Fire to Man

He stayed his colossal hand,
that craggy fist aflame with sun-spark,
and said,

> I have shattered the rules of Olympus,
> laid low god-law. How will you use
> what I give?

Man's red tongue kindled
and danced in the pyre of his lips.
He replied,

> I will batter down the godhead,
> crush the Thunderer's kin
> like a horse tramples snakes. I will smelt
>
> metals from the Earth, melt down
> the altars of gold, and I will rake
> from the ashes the secrets
>
> those deities jealously hoard. I will cast
> them like beggars into my street, and this world
> will be mine to inherit.

Tasting reprisal for his forebears'
defeat, the titan unfettered
the fire, unleashed it to Man, and whispered,

> Good.

The Wireless Deity

And here I pray my hands
will bend I bend my hands

in prayer to your blue face
your square portal unmoving

on my desk and dancing
around outside above

the prehistoric mist hanging
like a net over Madison Street

against the saurian neck
of the cherry picker booming

in the rain against the people
in its bucket or marching like beetles

in a small dark line to offices and
bars and you know where they are

you fly above them and nestle
in their pockets and headsets you

invisible ether unfelt ghost you brain
of atmosphere you electric dumb

speechless mouth you speak with
our words and you see our faces our

pasts our leftover dinners your
algorithms shift and nimble-flit

you're broadcasting me I'm receiving
you and I pray to break my hands

from your habit but your habit breaks
and bends my hands to prayer.

Aquarius' Age

Water-bearer, gild-boy
    reeking of rough sheep

and wild spelt. Gopherwood skin
    a bronze mirror for the Eagle

who snatched him, the feathered
    Fathergod whose lust crashed

like lightning amid the flock.
    And the presents plied to the parents,

stud stallions and diamond tankards
    to erase the boy's face, the lonely

abductee trafficked behind dark stars
    by a horny old god. See him

like a statue, slowly cracking
    amid all that cloud-white marble,

serving bubbling sap. Cup-carrier,
    servant, page, slave sent to draw water

from sacred wells long spoiled
    with oily plastic, BPAs, cyanide,

acid fish—awful offerings left by
    the flower children of the Summer of Love,

praying for the Age of Aquarius,
    stolen Ganymede. They never knew,

singing in the streets of San Francisco,
    their future children far from thought,

that he was really Isaac, betrayed
            and altar-bound. Or that they were

Abraham, ready for their lord
            with long and steely knives

that shone brighter, more beautiful
            than all the gods' jeweled goblets.

Perennial

They come every spring
      like little green snakes

that flower, later, their petaled suns.
      They beckon to the open spaces,

cast their scent the way
      gamblers throw dice.

Bees hover above them,
      hummingbirds flit to drink

from their long and pale necks.
      The sugar is swallowed, the wafer

eaten, and the illusion
      completed. The season's children

who sustain themselves—
      do they know that deep

within the barracks of soil,
      the perennials' gnarled truths

claw among eyeless worms?
      That they wait all winter,

like angler fish
      on the bottom of the ocean,

to dangle sweet lures
      above their sinister forms;

or like hucksters,
      their slogans at last in the headlines,

to sing out sweet promises
      they know they cannot keep?

Corpse Flower

Thick purple, dream-deep and breathing
        its dead-sweet air in a humid June hothouse,
bracing as the reality you finally taste
        the moment you ascend from sleeping. Months

later, a tawny supermoon was cut loose
        from evening's rust-bronze scrim, swelled
like a spiderbite on night's skin, and
        recalled that smell to my nostrils, that long-sleeping

scent known only after decades. Rare
        as the slow dust that orbits a collapsed house
like unsure and becalmed planets
        cusping the maw of a darkness

that stars used to light. And
        after late-autumn frost scrubbed the color
from the world, one fresh, pink
        magnolia blossom unfurled like a sail

from the top branch and drank
        the last, weak sunlight before browning
a day later and floating down to Earth
        like some withered angel, broken-winged

and confused. We will die so many
        deaths before we live. We will hum
in a slow, dead-sweet wind
        and the dream it roils within. And in a tall field

green with switchgrass, when
        sungold catches long shadows and pins
their wings to the evening, we'll count
        our losses, our gains, the day's remains.

Killing the Ants

Coal-dark little ants
       line the kitchen sink
like punctuation
       shaken from this poem
or the language of laws
       lifted from their bills
and exiled to die
       in shutdowns and legal hinterlands
miniscule reminders
       that fairness is a theory and
power necessitates weakness
       and we are all strangers
in strange houses
       like the man from the House
who says on tv
       he didn't actually read
the bill he passed he
       doesn't really know what
he does or why but
       the Party is strong
eternal and kinglike so
       forgive him these small faults
the small crumbs pecked
       like a kiss from your check
he's only trying to survive
       like the fleeing ants who smash
under my hand my flesh
       filling their terrible sky
forgive me I tell them
       I know not what I do

Alt-Reality

Like flies we cling to a world slap-flat
      disc-thin where bullets sing like schoolkids
hey-ho hey-ho
      where pizzamakers slice
their pepperoni bloody
      and bake sex slaves into the menu where
Earth and its mummy bones
      its carbon dating
          its wounded history
all fake news
      and trumped truths
coalsmoke clean as spring water
      runnels of oil like braided hair
where blossom-bruise
      where knuckle-kiss
          where bombs origami
      into heat and cloud wonderful
this beauty-town
      this godsent land
this chemtrail sky
      this jailhouse jaw
a vast and trembling carnage
this land was made
      for me
          me
              me

Politics in the Age of Poison

In a nightmare, the mouth unhinges

> like a door removing itself from a house
> where dinosaurs reconstruct themselves
> on live television to track blood
> down lumbering marble hallways
> and shout
> I am outraged
> and
> you are wrong and I am not
> and the door rattles and cracks and *rips*
> from its frame like dark-haired kids
> ripped from their homes
> and in the capitol the fangs come out

like a snake's to devour the body.

The Stripping Away

The quiet terror of leaves
        composting into brown soil,
of unseen microbes chittering
        their unheard liturgies. There
are vast, endless purgatories
        in the hollows of the body,
in the bared teeth of politicians,
        in restless hands that rush
like dogs through strange neighborhoods
        at night.

        An emptiness fills.
A hunger starves. From night's
        tall belltowers, there comes
a ringing that shakes the air
        in your eyelashes, the mites
dwelling within, the dark cells
        of their mandibles, the incalculable
voids swirling between their
        molecules. Nothing is solid—
not skin, clothes, lovingkindness,
        the despair of black mornings,
the joy of waking.

Even now, in a chamber
        far from here—in a courthouse,
a castle, a heart, who knows—
        something speaks your name
and does not know it.

Dream of the Black Sun

Shadows flood houses in a wet
and lightless surge. They lap against

sleeping eyelids, slip up nostrils
and paint visons of nuclear wind

in the skulls of those dreaming. I wear
a neighbor's hat like a lonely truth,

see their world's bright soil beneath
my dark sun. A snake bites the breast

of the eagle who is eating it. A city
pulses like a heart, crimson and deep

and crying angry, defiant songs. I
am blood in your vein, dark as rotten

wood. I am a hand that cannot close,
my voice an electricity thrumming

a thousand silent throats. When I awake,
my eyes are already open and full

of the black morning of my house,
sweet and bitter as what I can't see.

Divinity

Dionysius, mother-burned, drunk-struck,
      rambled insane through forests and moors.
Osiris, brother-killed, coffin-locked
      and dismembered, moldered in the Nile.
Odin made a gallows of the world,
      noosed himself and swung into darkness.
Buddha knew no peace
      until poverty and wilderness woke him.
Yahweh forged his own shadow,
      an ashy residue forever marring his creation.
Jesus was kissed and betrayed,
      spiked to a cross, left to die among thieves.
Muhammad heard the angel
      only in Hira's shadowy, glum solitude.
We see divinity in pain and loneliness
      wonder why our world bleeds so much.

God's Bucket List

Fold those yellow-dust pages
      of the holy writ you got all wrong
      into paper cranes, a flotilla
      of gunless destroyers. Sink
      them all with pennies and rocks.

Plant a forest of saplings,
      proudly measure their growth,
      sit in their cool shade.
      In their seventh year,
      hack them down.

Speak in actions only.
      Your vowels are wounds,
      your consonants are joys,
      your moments of silence
      are unimaginable horrors.

Find what you love best
      in the world. Wrap it
      in yesterday's newspaper,
      bury it in the winter woods,
      count the days until summer.

Stare into the eyes
      of a foreign woman.
      Do not look away
      until you've found
      your own fears and dreams.

Count all the colors
      burning the sky at sunset.
      Chant their names
      and know there are thousands more
      you'll never speak.

Grow and tend a garden.
      Raise and butcher an animal.
      Prepare the produce of both
      into savory and delicious meals.
      Let all of it rot.

Build a beautiful machine
      with a hundred moving parts.
      Give each part a dark fear
      and a secret hatred.
      Watch the machine implode.

Write a book,
      memorize every word,
      destroy the pages
      and recite it to strangers
      in bars after midnight.

Hitchhike all day
      and drive night.
      It does not matter to where.
      When the gas runs empty,
      get out and walk home.

Quit your job and sell your house.
      Live in the gutter
      with the homeless and the rats.
      Live miserably.
      Die slowly.

Sell apples by the roadside.
      When a person buys one,
      wash it, clean it,
      eat half in front of them.
      Tell them, *That's life.*

Sit naked

in a cage of starving lions.
Their roars will deafen you,
their jaws will consume you.
Let them.

Sisyphus at the Summit

The boulder crumbled eons ago—
even the gods can't defy erosion.

This is the question that rolled
like a dark ocean behind his eyes:

what happens when the Almighty's will
is bested by mere physics? Mortals weren't

supposed to reach the top. Men weren't
supposed to escape their punishments. But

all the Underworld's nebulous gloom swirled
below him, and his back was achingly unbent.

Like an eel through a net, he slipped out
of time, his mind a boat drifting on a starless sea,

waiting for someone to descend and tell
him it was all part of the plan. For the boulder

to reform like a cancer. For the mountain to rumble
and rear up to twice its height. Anything to keep

his ordeal eternal. He waited. And
waited.

                                   Finally,
he stood and wandered down the far side

of the mountain. Stretched his back, popped
his knuckles. Found the biggest boulder, the one

he imagined Zeus would have chosen. He planted
his feet, leaned hard against the stone. He thought

to push, but the wheel of habit had long ago snapped.
Slowly, he sat down in its shadow and did not get back up.

Is this part of it?

he asked the void.

He wasn't sure if anyone was listening anymore. But
he waited, still, for an answer.

IV.

Rejoining the Spiral

Speak of a Body

You speak of a body and conjure images
       of Tiananmen Square, or knives ladling
the human water from Caesar's chest, or
       the scalloped walls of an elected legislature.
Flesh and what darkness transpires—a
       nebular wellspring of violence, the iron
brutality of the mind's cathedrals.

You speak of a body and it scatters
       into a hive of ants, a murmuration
of starlings, a formless speckled cloud,
       a tangled mass of words. Indistinct
and rising upward, infectious, a bloom
       of algae reddening the fisherman's cove
and painting itself on the silver backs of sturgeons.

A ghost desires life. Matter disintegrates and
       reforms. The man who faced the tanks hovers
in hydrogen molecules near the sun. The last
       breath of the slain dictator right now swells
the lungs of a child eating ice cream on a bench
       down the street. She exhales, it slips away,
it mingles with sunlight, it ascends.

Links

Drumthump of drubbed blood
like timpani in the chest,
my pump pounding the same

        electric thunderstorm rhythms
        the priests of Ur and Babylon
        saw shaking the pillars of

the sycamore she sat beneath
in the autumn and heard
the cry of a bird that rang

        the doorbell and my father,
        age six, maybe opened the door
        and heard an ice cream truck

tolling like a funeral bell
for the poet whose signed book
I found tucked away beside

        a newspaper declaring
        the president was assassinated,
        another that two planes had

appeared dreamlike and
holy to your grandmother waiting
on the church steps for

        when the Nazis marched in Nuremberg,
        Warsaw, Paris, Madison-Square Garden,
        Skokie, Charlottesville

where a student recites
Wilfred Owens' poetry and
envisions a graveyard stretching

in the morning, bacon sizzling
and coffee brewing and a cat purring
at the foot of your bed

and the moment stretches, bleeds
into others, becomes them, one moment,
one, eternity in a breath, breathe, one.

Becoming Rain

The sky bends low and rakes us
with clouds the way a monk furrows
his garden. The rain is warm

and slips like pearls
down my wife's neck. I imagine
the rain soaking through us,

flooding our veins
with the scent of wet summer grass.
We drove for hours once,

following the moon like
a breath after a song, and
the same moon now curves

in the sky like a tumbled cup,
spilling its drink everywhere.
The rain fills us, hears

our names in our heartbeats,
tastes our slow inner oceans.
It moves our feet, clasps

our hands, we wade through
a culvert and our socks cling
to our ankles like barnacles to a ship,

we evaporate beneath streetlamps, we melt
on a pile of soaked clothes, we steam upward
like the gaze of transfixed prophets.

In a Previous Life

Steam rose from black farmfields
in the velvet before sunbreak. And when
frost glittered like sweat

on the shadow-bark of wild orchards,
I was there to see its glint. Dirt clung
in the caves of my chests, my feet

dug and rooted and drank
from nameless underground rivers.
I pushed plows down the ditches

of my legs. I swung from trees
and ate their apples, sank my axes
into their trunks and danced

on their shorn stumps. And when
night's coals scattered like heartbeats
above the mountains, I drank

the moon's sweet and sleepy milk,
uncorked oceans that only ever knew
their dark bottles. I died young—snuffed

out by a fever that slipped its fire
into me like a star skipping
across the night sky.

In Praise of Life

O Death you singer and all-maker
you all-shaper you laughing
child-light that busts down night's
doors you sweet-song lullabying
and gentle-sighing through the grasses
I sit down among you snap you
pull me from bed and chant cloud-trails
that trace only once the loving curls
of instants I smell the sweetness you've
brewed in the wildflowers I hear
your name in the grackle's chatter and
in the hawk's swooping glide and
in the million-million chirp-howls
of night-bugs in summer heat and
I know I'll hear you one day whistling
outside my window and we'll go for a stroll
and I'll know at last where you settle
and dwell in what yellow-green field
you dream under what moon-sun
you rise and fall I'll know then but
until then I'll walk the paths where
you've been before and will be again.

Tree Bones

Planked and bundled, scraps and shims.
            Plane them smooth and clean, trim

the edges and knobs. Pine curlings
            like ocean waves flowing down my arm,

arbor dust like spilled flour on my boots.
            Heartwood in my hands, limbs and roots,

woodgrains a calligraphy unfurling
            along a sawblade. Varnishes to embalm

what grows no more, to strengthen
            old tree bones and lengthen

their use. Gluing, nailing, learning
            how broken bits can be voiceless psalms—

reborn, formed, and joined to something new.
            I can only hope my own bones find such use.

Half-dream in Autumn

        I awoke in the dream and heard
dawn's haze-gold slowly

        wrapping itself around the curves
of the mulberry trees, running

        its fingers through emerald leaves,
smoldering, crisping, burning.

        And I was there—outside in
a grass-lake, green-kneeling

        beneath a rolling sun and
harvesting the water funneling

        like a whisper from our garden.
There was a word, a sound

        spelled in the snowflake writ
of clematis petals drifting

        like geese across a copper sky.
Like raindrops arranged

        to a hymn. And it was gone
as soon as it was uttered.

Driving on an August Evening

Cicada's hacksaw jabber storming
        the air of Highway 46, tree-song
and dusk-wind and engine-hum,
        Brown County's sunset burning
behind us, the clouds fire-misty
        and smoking like barges steaming
for westward ports, the night
        ignited, her eyes afire her
smile wide the pines melting
        against that deep Rothko sky—
berries, bonfires, red lips, gold corn.

On a Ferry for Beaver Island, MI

The horizon a smooth edge
      of a turquoise bowl,
            waves of crumpled paper.

            Azure bliss of namelessness,
      wave-carried beneath the clouded dome.
The world a simplicity of blue and white,

and, beyond,
      a growing beach of green.

Greening

Dark clouds burst
  from around the sun like
a shout like a flock
  of dispersing magpies like

a trumpet-blast as though
  the winged myths of the Euphrates
have cracked their chains
  but fables are unreal and

unlike the grasses that cradle
  your crown your skull your thoughts
that drift in the dandelion fluff
  and name the scutch the fescue

the crab and rye the smooth or
  toothy or pinnate or compound you
know the life-spans of like
  a favorite rhyme they wind-speak

and confirm we ourselves are
  poems stressed and metrical composed
in atomic languages in an endless
  meadow of all things a field like

the one in which we once were
  taught to consider lilies and mustard
seeds but the green weave beneath
  you hums so healthy and diverse and

stronger than you or
  churchyards or temples and it sings
hallelujah o holy sweet wind
  it grows
    it grows
      it grows.

Samuel T. Franklin studied History and English at Indiana State University, where he earned a Bachelor's in one and a Master's in the other. He is the author of a previous poetry collection, *The God of Happiness* (Main Street Rag, 2016). A 2018 Best of the Net nominee, his poems have appeared in such publications as *Riggwelter, Rabid Oak, The Indianapolis Review*, and *Hoosier Lit.*

Currently a content developer, Samuel has previously found work as an adjunct lecturer, a tutor, a grounds crew member, and a produce clerk, among other things. He and his wife live in Bloomington, Indiana. Samples of his work can be read online at www.samueltfranklin.com.

www.ingramcontent.com/pod-product-compliance
Lightning Source LLC
Chambersburg PA
CBHW021154090426
42740CB00008B/1088